ACHIEVE FINANCIAL FREEDOM

THE ROAD MAP TO FINANCIAL SUCCESS

MARIA L. ELLIS, MBA

Difference Press

Washington, DC, USA

Published 2020

DISCLAIMER

No part of this publication may be reproduced or transmitted in any form or by any means, mechanical or electronic, including photocopying or recording, or by any information storage and retrieval system, or transmitted by email without permission in writing from the author.

Neither the author nor the publisher assumes any responsibility for errors, omissions, or contrary interpretations of the subject matter herein. Any perceived slight of any individual or organization is purely unintentional.

Brand and product names are trademarks or registered trademarks of their respective owners.

This book is designed to provide basic information that the author believes to be accurate on the subject matter it covers, but it is sold with the understanding that neither the author nor the publisher is offering individualized advice tailored to any specific portfolio or to any individual's particular needs, or rendering investment, legal, or accounting advice.

No warranty is made with respect to the accuracy or completeness of the information contained herein, and both the author and the publisher specifically disclaim any responsibility for any liability, loss, or risk, personal or otherwise, which is

Cover Design: Nakita Duncan

ADVANCE PRAISE

"Achieving financial freedom is the path to control your life's destiny in terms of creating success and self-happiness. Being a Vietnamese woman living in Australia, I endured hard work to achieve my own financial freedom and success. The book is well-written and designed to help women of all ages to understand and implement their path to financial freedom."

— LE HOA WYSHAM, REAL ESTATE INVESTOR, MANAGING DIRECTOR, MCDONALDRE.CO

"I have raised three smart and curious daughters to adulthood and self-dependence. When they were young, I went through years ruminating over their imminent foray into the big world. How much smoother would the ride have been with this remarkable book in hand.

Kudos to the author for an incisive and ingenious account to liberate women with financial clout."

— DR. GUNA THEESAN, REAL ESTATE INVESTOR

"You make the path to success for women so clear and concise. Financial freedom is the first step for all women, of all ages, to achieve to ultimately control our destiny."

— HSH PRINCESS RITA BONCOMPAGNI LUDOVISI, PRINCIPESSA DI PIOMBINO XII

"If I had read this book when I was young and ignorant about money and investing, I would have avoided mistakes that I am sure are common even among today's more sophisticated millennials."

— DINNI GORDON, PROFESSOR EMERITA, COLLEGE UNIVERSITY OF NEW YORK

"This book represents a new paradigm for women and girls interested in achieving financial freedom. It provides the starting point to act and move toward becoming a financially-successful future self."

— BENJAMIN HARDY,
ORGANIZATIONAL PSYCHOLOGIST,
AND NEW YORK TIMES BESTSELLING
AUTHOR OF *WILLPOWER DOESN'T
WORK AND PERSONALITY ISN'T
PERMANENT*

"To succeed, women need to have a vision. This book is a must-read for every Gen X and millennial woman, showing a clear path to financial independence and how to build a bold vision for the future."

— NADA MARIE ANID, PHD, VICE
PRESIDENT OF STRATEGIC
COMMUNICATIONS AND EXTERNAL
AFFAIRS, FORMER DEAN OF
ENGINEERING AT NEW YORK
INSTITUTE OF TECHNOLOGY, AND CO-
EDITOR OF *THE INTERNET OF WOMEN:
ACCELERATING CULTURE CHANGE*

"Understanding financial concepts is important to successfully manage one's life. It is often a missing piece, especially for women who are socialized to believe the financial world is the purview of men. It is the purview of everyone, and this book goes a long way to making that a reality. I am so pleased that Maria, a former banker, has written this highly readable book which will help so many. I'm also pleased that she is generously donating all proceeds to the AAUW to promote education for all girls and women. Thank you, Maria."

— KATHRYN SWINTEK, MANAGING PARTNER, GOLDEN SEEDS FUND 2, LP

"I encourage every person I teach, coach and lead to pursue financial wealth. Money allows us to give to those in need and to make our family's dreams come true. But, it's crucial to keep in mind that money follows core rules. Learning and understanding those rules is the first step toward achieving financial growth, security, and ultimately independence. Ellis presents solid, fundamental, easy to understand guidance for women of all ages who want to be educated about money in the pursuit of financial freedom. If you want to change the world, go make money. It's not about the money. It's about what the money can do."

— MO ANDERSON, VICE CHAIRMAN OF THE BOARD AND CO-OWNER OF KELLER WILLIAMS REALTY INTERNATIONAL

"Maria Ellis offers a readable primer – an introduction to the complexities of personal finance and retirement planning. An added benefit based on Maria's personal experience: a guide to navigating some of the distinctive challenges women face as they try to maximize their well-being in a culture prone to minimize their opportunities."

— CHARLES L. FLYNN, JR., COLLEGE OF MOUNT SAINT VINCENT

CONTENTS

FOREWORD

Maria Ellis has written a book about a topic that is always important, generation after generation: how to ensure that your personal financial management enhances your efforts and achievements in all other aspects of your life. Maria spent her entire career in the financial world, rising up the ladder at a bank conducting international business and now in real estate. She deeply understands financial concepts and has given the gift of sharing her knowledge and expertise in a highly readable book. Modular in format, *Achieve Financial Freedom* starts with the basics, which is your budget and your long-term financial goals. Maria explains how anyone can – and should – create a personal financial budget to start with, create a strong foundation for successfully managing in the present and preparing for the future you want. Chock full of helpful references to additional resources in each chapter, you, the reader, can decide where you want to dive deeper.

Maria's life story is inspiring. Immigrating to the United States with her family after graduating from high school in Guayaquil, Ecuador, where she was born and spent her formative years, Maria pursued her BBA and MBA at the University of Massachusetts, and later enrolled in the Harvard Business School Owner-President Management program. This education allowed Maria to pursue her professional dreams and is a great example of one of the three pillars in successful personal financial management which are: saving, investing, and education. Regardless of your own individual professional pursuits, seeking out opportunities to add to your knowledge in your field pays lifetime dividends both monetarily and in your sense of self-worth and confidence.

I am so proud of Maria's work with the American Association of University Women, offering classes on personal financial management and on salary negotiation to college women. *Achieve Financial Freedom* builds on these foundational tools and can serve as a helpful reference guide as you reach each of your personal and personal financial milestones. I should add that Maria possesses a great work ethic; she commits to doing her best in all that she takes on. In addition to her real estate and advisory business, Maria is a pro-bono consultant with the Harvard Business School Club of New York's Community

Partners whose mission is to create constructive partnerships between Harvard Business School alumni and nonprofit organizations in the greater New York City metropolitan area that seek assistance with business and management issues. And after all, every initiative and project are a learning opportunity.

Like Maria, I am a former banker. For the last ten years, I have been an investor in startup companies and serve as a director of several corporations. Just as in personal financial management, successful startup companies start with a detailed budget that puts into dollars and cents their vision of how they plan to change the world – how much money do they have to spend? What should they spend it on? If you want to know the answers to these important questions as applied to your life, Maria's book will help you to find them.

— Kathryn Swintek, managing partner of Golden Seeds Fund 2

1

IF I AM SO SMART, WHY CAN'T I ACHIEVE FINANCIAL FREEDOM?

A few years ago, I met with Ms. Maven, an executive working in a highly competitive investment banking firm in New York City. She had been working in investment banking for ten years and her job required her to effectively identify, monitor, and evaluate the company's financial and operating risks. Her career was male-dominated, and she was one of the few executive women at the company. In addition to her risk-management functions, her position also required her to travel outside the New York City area to recruit talent for her department.

Ms. Maven's career was highly visible. It required long hours and it was highly stressful. Therefore, she had no free time for herself; however, she made time to attend meetings that were in alignment with her desire to promote education for women and girls.

She liked to encourage girls and young women to follow their passions because when she was in seventh grade her teacher told her that "girls are not good in math" and therefore, she should not bother studying math. It was then that Ms. Maven decided that she was going to prove her math teacher wrong; she went on to love math and obtain a PhD in mathematics.

Ms. Maven lived in Manhattan in a small apartment, and her biggest challenge was to make progress on her financial freedom. She was now thirty-five years old and hoping to find her ideal partner, but she had not yet found the right person, someone who had values and a striving career that she approved of. She just did not have the time though, because her career was highly visible and well paid but all came at a high price. She was concerned that if she lost her job, she would not be able to pay her living expenses. However, if Ms. Maven learned how to put her financial affairs in order and to save and invest her money, she would be able to spend more time in her personal life and achieve her life vision and financial freedom. For Ms. Maven, financial freedom means having enough money to be able to buy a one-bedroom condo apartment instead of renting a small studio apartment in New York City, enjoying more free time to be able to take a vacation, and even perhaps finding the love of her life, her ideal partner to enjoy life with.

As you read this book, you may realize that you are in the same position as Ms. Maven. Therefore, you too will have to initiate some soul-searching steps in order to achieve financial freedom. You will need to consider making some internal and external adjustments such as creating a budget, minimizing your expenses, negotiating a better salary and greater benefits, asking for a promotion, or seeking a higher-paying job. I decided to become a salary negotiation facilitator because I did not have a mentor to guide me early in my life. I know I could have achieved financial freedom sooner if I had had proper guidance. In my experience as a coach and facilitator for the American Association of University Women (AAUW) teaching salary negotiation to college graduates at the New York Institute of Technology and at The New School in New York City, I found that women and girls do not know how best to negotiate and ask for a competitive salary, which would provide them with an increased income to help them pay off their student debt much quicker and provide them with extra funds to start their financial planning to become financially independent.

When you are negotiating a salary for your first job and/or a promotion with your new or current employer, you must know your personal value and what makes you different from other potential candidates, like that you speak different languages. For instance, I was able to obtain work to put myself through college because I was fluent in Spanish, and an international company needed a person to translate their operating manuals for their clients in Latin America.

Your employer needs you as much as you need them, and you need to tell your employer how you bring value to the growth of the company: share with them what skills, accomplishments, and work experiences demonstrate the value or contribution you might make in the position or the promotion you are applying for and provide specific examples. You must research and identify comparable job titles, find a market rate for the position you are applying for, and establish your target salary range. It is important that you know your target salary and benefits and know your strategy to negotiate and have a win-win outcome. For more information about salary negotiation, go to this link: https://www.aauw.org/resources/programs/salary/.

One of my goals is for you to recognize your value and the skillset that you bring to your potential employer and to help you achieve a competitive salary and benefits package. Whether it is negotiating for your salary or knowing how much money you need to cover your living expenses and start achieving your financial objectives, you need to know how to research your target salary and negotiate it by highlighting your skillset and your accomplishments. My goal is to help accomplish our AAUW mission to advance gender equity for women and girls through research, education, and advocacy. Our vision, equity for all, can and must be achieved. Therefore, all proceeds from this book will be donated to AAUW.

After graduating from college, I wanted to earn money and become financially independent, but I did not know how to go about it. Also, even though I worked on a part-time basis throughout my college years, I still had college loans with high interest rates. I sought advice from educated friends who advised me to put aside money to start a savings account. If I knew then what I know now, I would have paid my college loan first because the interest rates are always higher than the interest earned in a savings account. I am writing this book with much love and gratitude and have developed a road map to help you achieve financial freedom.

Once you have negotiated a competitive salary, whether you do it yourself or hire a financial advisor, you will be in a unique position to create and review on a quarterly basis your complete financial picture. Your financial plan is a fluid and flexible document that changes over time as your life priorities change. Reviewing your complete financial picture includes doing an asset allocation analysis to identify any red flags like overconcentration in a particular investment or industry sector, doing a personal risk assessment and making sure that your portfolio is in sync with your feelings about risk, analyzing whether or not you need some specialized assistance with estate or taxing planning, and determining whether your current savings plan will achieve your financial objectives, and if not, helping you create an action plan to get you on track.

In the specific case of Ms. Maven, who lived in Manhattan in a small apartment and whose biggest challenge was to make progress on her personal life and financial freedom, she too will have to create and implement her financial plan to enable her to enjoy her life's vision and financial freedom.

2

WHY IS ACHIEVING FINANCIAL FREEDOM IMPORTANT?

"When you change the way you look at things, the things you look at change."

— DR. WAYNE DYER

This book is meant to provide you with a basic road map to make you aware of various investment alternatives and financial tools to help you achieve financial freedom, but before I do that, I want to share with you my background and experience in life so far. Well, I am originally from Guayaquil, Ecuador. I am one of five siblings – three brothers, Francisco, Sergio, and Ruben, and my sister, Zulema. As the oldest child, I always felt responsible for the well-being of my Spanish family. After graduating from high school, Colegio 28 de Mayo in Guayaquil, my loving parents (mostly my wise mother, Jenny) were convinced that leaving Ecuador and coming to the United States would offer their children a future.

Consequently, we moved to New York in 1970. Upon arrival, I started working at a small company near our new home in Chelsea. Shortly thereafter, I decided to go to college and graduated from the University of Massachusetts in Amherst with a Bachelor of Business Administration. My dearest hope was to start a career at one of the major banks in New York City. After various job interviews, I knew that in order to achieve my career goal to become a vice president of the bank, I needed to obtain my Master's Degree in Business Administration, so I decided to continue my studies and obtain an MBA.

In 1976, after receiving my MBA, a global bank hired me to provide financing to their international corporate clients who were exporting goods and services to Latin America. With Spanish as my first language, I felt right at home and was happy to have accomplished this career goal on a timely basis. As my friends know, I am a goal-driven woman, so I became a vice president. At age twenty-nine, I found the love of my life, Steve, to whom I have been married for over forty years and with whom I have two wonderful sons, Michael and Tommy. As of this writing, I am even a grandmother. My beautiful granddaughter's name is Maven.

At this point in my life, per Maslow's hierarchy of

needs, I had addressed my physiological needs, safety needs, love/belonging needs, and esteem needs, and now I was working on my self-actualization. Maslow emphasized the importance of self-actualization, which is a process of growing and developing as a person in order to achieve individual potential. At the peak of Maslow's hierarchy are the self-actualization needs. "What a man can be, he must be," Maslow explained, referring to the need people have to achieve their full potential as human beings.

I am now making progress and enjoying self-actualization. I love to have peak experiences where I emerge feeling changed and transformed. For example, my volunteer work to promote education for women and girls has changed and transformed me over the years. I enjoy self-acceptance and accepting others as the gift that we represent to the world.

I enjoy viewing life as it unfolds, logically, rationally, and emotionally. For instance, I provide pro bono consulting and business advice to local nonprofit organizations through well-defined consulting projects. I tend to be solution-centered, not focusing on daily challenges but instead focusing on the joyful expansion of creation.

I adore being autonomous. I live in the moment and appreciate the beauty of my daily experiences. Some of my most recent experiences have been traveling to places around the world, including listening to great opera in Bulgaria, drinking cool mineral water from natural water springs in Sofia, being inspired by Rome's stunning architecture (the Coliseum, Pantheon, and Trevi Fountain), and exploring the Vatican City and being spiritually moved by the history and beauty of St. Peter's Basilica, the Sistine Chapel, and the Vatican Museums.

I enjoy my solitude and privacy. While I enjoy the company of others, I always seek to take time for myself and enjoy nurturing the love that my inner being offers to me. My inner being is like an oasis in the desert. One of my most precious memories is of taking time to enjoy a sunrise and taking a private yoga lesson at Lodhi Garden while visiting friends in New Delhi. Lodhi Garden is one of the oldest gardens in the world. Built in the fifteenth century and covering ninety acres of land, this park holds tombs of two emperors of Delhi: Lodhi and Shah. I felt transported to a mystical world when visiting Udaipur, the City of Lakes. Serene Udaipur is the crowning jewel of royal Rajasthan. With shimmering lakes visible from almost every rooftop, fairytale palaces, sprawling Havelis, revered temples, and narrow lanes weaving through colorful markets as ancient as the city's history, Udaipur's charm is unmatched.

One of my most enjoyable traits is my sense of humor. My friends and I love to tell stories and laugh often. Spontaneity is my strength and I enjoy being open, unconventional, and spontaneous. Yes, I fully enjoy the journey, not just the destination.

According to Maslow's Hierarchy of Needs, Self-actualizing people are concerned with personal growth, less concerned with the opinions of others, and interested in fulfilling their potential. If you are wondering why I am sharing these experiences with you, it is because financial freedom enables you to have these memorable experiences in your life's journey.

3

THE ROAD TO FINANCIAL FREEDOM

"There is no degree for 'live your dreams.' You qualify yourself by showing up and working. You get permission by deciding."

— DR. BENJAMIN HARDY

The purpose of this chapter is to share investment strategies to achieve financial freedom. Investing is easy once you learn the investment principles and you are committed to investing for your financial well-being; however, your most challenging part is for you to belief that you can and will succeed in achieving financial freedom. Remember that decisions, not conditions, determine your destiny. You must focus and take control of your finances. You will learn that one of the most important steps on the road to financial freedom is to create a specific investment strategy unique to your financial well-being. Before you dive into the process itself, it is important for you to explore the context behind the process and what exactly you will be doing to achieve financial freedom.

I have purposefully not written a long and comprehensive textbook for you. Instead, it is more like a quick guide to help you start on your journey to achieving financial freedom to enable you to live your dream life. In this book, you will learn how to create a road map to financial success. In Chapter 4, you will start by thinking about how best to create a comprehensive financial plan that is the right financial plan for you at this point in time in your life journey. You will create an annual budget detailing all your income, expenses, and specific amounts to be set aside for monthly investments. You will think about where you feel comfortable making changes and brainstorm about all your recurring expenses that you could eliminate or reduce to enable you to have more money to save and start investing. I encourage you to work with a fiduciary advisor to help you create short-term and long-term financial objectives, including a portfolio growth strategy based on your risk tolerance and time horizon.

In Chapter 5, you will learn that an investment portfolio is composed of stocks, bonds, and cash.

Your investment strategy will guide you in your day-to-day decisions on investment.

In Chapter 6, you will learn about investing in aggressive stocks with high growth and risk potential as well as bonds with high yield and risk potential. You can invest in stocks, bonds, or mutual funds and you may consider either managing your money or consulting with a fiduciary advisor to guide you in this process.

In Chapter 7, you will learn about alternative investments for your portfolio, including real estate and precious metals like gold and silver. There are two reasons to invest in alternative assets: volatility and diversity.

In Chapter 8, you will learn about homeownership, which is a useful way to invest and build equity. There are various ways to invest in real estate to build equity and create cash flow. For instance, owning rental properties is a good way to create additional income and defer capital gains. This chapter will talk about large real estate investors and entrepreneurs investing in real estate including multi-family, office, industrial, and retail space.

In Chapter 9, you will learn about investment alternatives when planning for retirement. Before you begin planning for retirement, you need to consider how much money you will need to live your dream life. You will need to make some assumptions as to the length of your retirement years and create a realistic budget and investment plan for unforeseeable situations such as sickness.

In Chapter 10, you will learn to manage your retirement account, including annuities and long-term care. Annuities provide you the opportunity to grow your future income while also offering options to help protect against inflation and market downturns. Long-term care covers long-term care services including custodial care.

In Chapter 11, you will learn about the advantages and disadvantages of life insurance. The motivation behind life coverage is to give monetary assurance to your surviving dependents. Therefore, it is essential to investigate your desired lifestyle and budgetary circumstances before buying life insurance protection.

In Chapter 12, I would love to help you create the grandest possible vision for all aspects of your life and your future self, including health and fitness, career, financial, social, intellectual, emotional, character, spiritual, love relationships, parenting, and stewardship. According to research done by Dr. Daniel Gilbert of Harvard, people are bad at predicting who they will be in the future. The reason is simple: it is far easier to remember the past than to imagine the future. Professor Gilbert is interested in how human beings navigate the complexities of time and social life.

The first of these interests motivates his research on affective forecasting (how and how well people can predict the emotional consequences of future events), inter-temporal choice (when and how people sacrifice for the future), and other topics in judgment and decision making.

Dr. Benjamin Hardy, organizational psychologist and New York Times bestselling author of Willpower Doesn't Work and Personality Isn't Permanent, encourages people to look at their present and future selves as two different people; your likelihood of making better decisions here and now will improve. The only way to create confidence is by pursuing what you have never done before. Following Dr. Hardy's advice, when preparing your financial plan, envision the successful person you want to be, your future self, and plan accordingly.

As Dan Sullivan, founder of Strategic Coach, said, "Personal confidence comes from making progress toward goals that are far bigger than your present capabilities." If you want to have financial freedom, you must create a financial plan and anticipate what is to come and how you can achieve your overall financial objectives. Let us start by imagining who you want to be in three to five years. What is your vision for your future? You cannot achieve financial freedom without knowing your starting point and your destination. Identifying how much obligation you have, what investment funds you're lacking, and how much cash you need can be a discouraging reality. In any case, this is an important positive development.

A decent spot to begin is to assemble a rundown of every one of your obligations: contracts, loan advances, vehicle advances, charge cards, or other obligations you may have assumed. Remember to incorporate any cash you may have acquired from companions or relatives throughout the years. A home loan can be considered a good obligation. You have to live someplace, and a month-to-month apartment lease is simply lost cash. A great many people purchase a home, and they trust that the home will increase in value after more than seven years. There is no assurance of this, obviously. Home loans often have low-financing costs when contrasted with credit cards – another explanation for why they are a case of good obligation.

As of now, in spring 2020, it is conceivable to obtain a mortgage under 4 percent, a truly low percentage for a long-term mortgage loan. Additionally, you should arrange a rundown of every one of your assets including your bank accounts, stocks, bonds, and retirement funds. Also add any additional income such as salary, stock dividends, etc. To experience financial freedom, you are going to need to look at money as a tool to help you achieve your dreams, fuel your energy, and live a stress-free life you can enjoy.

It is important to write down your short, intermediate, and long-term financial life goals. Why do you want to achieve financial freedom? Are you planning to pay off your college debt, save money for a wedding, traveling, retirement? You must write down your specific and obtainable financial and personal goals that you can measure and a time frame to accomplish them. For instance, you might want to pay off $30,000 in student loans and save $100,000 for a memorable wedding, $75,000 to travel around the world, and $800,000 for retirement.

Saving money consistently is important; it is also important to track your monthly spending. It is critical that you pay yourself first, meaning that you set aside a specific amount of money on a monthly basis. In Chapters 4 to 12 you will learn about various investing and retirement plans and, ultimately, the things that will help you live a more fulfilled life. Achieving financial freedom enables you to enjoy life's precious moments with family and friends. According to Gordon Livingston, MD, humans need three things to be happy: something to do, someone to love, and something to look forward to. If you do not have something to look forward to, for which you are exerting conscious and daily effort to create, then you cannot have happiness.

"Where there is no vision, the people perish," the Bible states. At the point when you make a new vision for your life, you quickly start to see through the viewpoint of that new vision. It turns into an amazing new setting and changes the context of your life. Changing the context changes the meaning and possibility. You simply want to get very clear on what you want three years from now. So, pull out your calendar and put a big X three to five years in the future. What does your life look like? What do you look like? What does your environment look like? Who are the main people in your life? What is the overall experience you are having? What does your typical day look like? How much money are you making? What is important to you? Where is your focus?

When you have created the future vision of yourself, share it with your family and friends and become responsible for achieving your life vision. Hearing yourself say it will cause you to believe it more – your thoughts should become words, words should become courageous actions, actions habits, and habits your personality and destiny. When you begin making powerful decisions in your life, you are then enabled to prioritize your life and determine your desired outcome.

According to Dan Sullivan, there are four steps to create breakthrough results. Dan calls it the 4 Cs Formula:

- Commitment: If you want to achieve

financial well-being, you must be committed and start today. I encourage you to take a leap of faith and start your road to your financial freedom now.

- Courage: Most individuals appreciate mental fortitude in others yet don't care for the experience themselves. For the vast majority, comprehending what to do isn't the issue. Getting the chance to do it long enough for results to show is the test. In general, we tend to have difficulties in one area or another. For a few, it might be adhering to a budget or a financial objective. You must have the courage to make a commitment to your financial well-being. Therefore, you must create a financial plan based on your vision and desired quality of life.
- Confidence: The new degree of certainty you experience after a breakthrough is the thing that enables you to focus on a much greater achievement and a significantly more prominent feeling of certainty. Life is uncertain; however, you must have the courage to dream big and create big opportunities for yourself even if you don’t have all the answers at that particular moment in time.
- Capability: Think back to one of your

> forward leaps. Wasn't it the blend of making a commitment and experiencing a period requiring a ton of mental fortitude that made both the new capacity and the new certainty? Now you have an opportunity to create your financial plan that will propel your current financial situation to a whole new level. Believing that you can achieve financial freedom is the first step. Ask yourself a transformation question: "What if there were no barriers and I could achieve anything?"

Once you see that you can accomplish the quality of life that you created in your life vision, you then must start believing that you can achieve it. With the right state of mind, desire, and determination, you will start by creating a comprehensive financial plan and applying investment strategies shared in Chapters 4 to 12, including investment portfolio and capital appreciation, investing in aggressive stocks with high growth, bonds with high yield potential, alternative investments suitable to your portfolio, and investing in real estate. As time passes and your financial needs change, you will know how to best select the investments and estate planning tools that are appropriate for you at each stage of your life, including balancing your investment portfolio, minimizing your taxes, and investing and managing your retirement account, annuities, and long-term care insurance.

4

A COMPREHENSIVE FINANCIAL PLAN

To start your financial planning, you will need to create both short- and long-term financial objectives based on your risk tolerance and time horizon.

You must begin with an end in mind by creating an annual budget, detailing all your income and expenses, and designating specific amounts to be set aside for monthly investments. Here are types of investments that you will want to consider as you launch your financial planning and build a portfolio:

- Investing monthly: This is highly recommended if you want to build and grow an investment portfolio. Your short-term investment portfolio should have six to twelve months of cash to cover emergencies and/or unforeseeable circumstances such as becoming ill or losing a job. One of my clients recently lost her job and she was able to use the funds available in her short-term portfolio to cover her living expenses while she looked for another job opportunity.

- Short-term investment alternatives offer liquidity: Some deposit accounts let you access your money immediately, although they may charge a penalty for early withdrawal. What's more, some investments are simpler to exchange into hard cash than others. Be that as it may, these ventures don't shield you from inflation, which has averaged around 3 percent in the course of the last twenty-five or more years. Investing money consistently includes some level of risk, regardless of how little. Yet, when you do not invest, you don't risk loss; you guarantee it. Some of the safest short-term investments include high-yield savings. Savings accounts are insured by the federal government through the Federal Deposit Insurance Corporation (FDIC). Your first $250,000 is secure. Most banks pay nothing or basically nothing on savings accounts; however, some banks offer a higher yearly rate contingent upon current rates. For example, a twelve-month Certificate of Deposit (CD) offers a higher rate. Ask your bank what the current rates are for Money Market Accounts (MMAs), and find out what the withdrawal restrictions are. Treasury Bills are fixed income investments, sold by the US Treasury with maturity periods extending from a couple of days to as long as a year. The greater the maturity, the higher the interest rate.

- Additionally, consider investing in Treasury Inflation Protected Securities (TIPS) to shield you from inflation. TIPS are a type of Treasury security issued by the US government that is indexed to inflation to protect investors from a decline in the purchasing power of their money. As inflation rises, TIPS adjust in price to maintain their real value.

Exchange-traded funds (ETFs) hold assets such as stocks, bonds or commodities and they are low-cost investments traded on stock exchanges. Bond ETFs are a type of exchange-traded fund (ETF) that exclusively invests in bonds. These are similar to bond mutual funds because they hold a portfolio of bonds with different strategies, maturity dates and the yields vary accordingly.

A mutual fund is an open-end professionally managed investment fund that pools money from many investors to purchase securities. Long-term mutual funds offer diversification and opportunity to grow your portfolio. There are many types of mutual fund investment opportunities that you can select, again depending on your risk profile and time horizon. Check your portfolio at least once a year. If your current asset mix differs from your target by five percentage points or more, rebalance. Portfolio rebalancing is the process of making changes in your existing portfolio so that it matches the currently recommended/desired portfolio for you.

There are many other categories of mutual funds including a) equity funds, invested in stocks that are either actively or passively managed and are categorized by industry, geography, etcetera; b) balanced or hybrid funds, invested in both equity and debt instruments; c) index funds or exchanged-traded funds, tracking a specified basket of underlying investments such as the S&P 500 or the Dow Jones Industrial Average; and, d) specialty mutual funds, invested in securities of a particular industry, sector, type of security, or geographic region. Which of these funds is best for your portfolio depends on your overall financial objectives.

The more youthful you are, the more your portfolio ought to incorporate equity funds, as you have more opportunity to adjust to the inescapable ups and downs in the market value. Equity mutual funds offer portfolio diversification in different ways relying upon the objectives of the funds. Some funds focus on large-caps, mid-caps, and small-cap companies, which refer to the company's market capitalization:

- Large-cap fund: companies with a market estimation of more than $10 billion
- Mid-cap fund: companies worth $2 billion to $10 billion
- Small-cap fund: companies worth $300 million to $2 billion

Industry or sector funds are centered around specific industries such as technology innovation, oil and gas, aeronautics, or health care. For example, investors who want exposure to gains by companies like Google and Apple could invest in a technology fund. Ownership in various sector funds can help differentiate your portfolio, so if one industry is hit hard (like the dot-com stocks in 2000), those losses can be counterbalanced by gains in different sectors of the economy.

Growth and value funds are another mutual fund differentiator. Growth funds look for stocks that fund managers believe will have superior returns. Value funds search for organizations whose stock is underestimated by the market.

International, global, and emerging market funds can likewise decide how a mutual fund can be composed. For instance, international funds invest in companies doing business outside the US while global funds put resources into organizations working in the United States and abroad. Emerging market funds target countries with small but developing markets.

Bond funds are the most common type of fixed income mutual funds. Rather than buying stocks, bond funds invest in government and corporate bonds. Investors approaching retirement age often have a large percentage of their portfolio invested in bond funds. As you approach your retirement, you will need a predictable income, and one of the classic ways to receive continual cash flow from investments is to set up a bond ladder, a bond investment with different maturity dates. You can invest in individual bonds, certificates of deposit, and exchange-traded funds with different maturity dates to allow you to anticipate an income stream from your fixed-income portfolio. Vanguard founder Jack Bogle suggests buying into low-cost, low-fee bond index funds that spread out your risk because you will own every part of the bond market.

Money market mutual funds are fixed-income funds that invest in short-term debt from governments, banks, or companies. These funds include assets such as US Treasury bills, certificates of deposit, and commercial paper. They are viewed as the safest investments and make up 15 percent of the mutual funds available in the marketplace. The income generated from these investments is either tax-exempt or taxable, depending on the specific investment. All mutual funds comply with the federal regulations based on quality, maturity, liquidity, credit quality, and diversification.

Balanced or hybrid funds are a blend of equity and fixed-income assets with a fixed percentage of investments. For example, a conservative fund would be composed of 65 percent stocks and 35 percent bonds. The equity portion offers capital appreciation while the debt portion offers security. One of the most popular balanced or hybrid funds are target funds, which reallocate the percentage of equity to bonds the closer you get to your retirement. Target funds can be conservative, moderate, or aggressive depending on the nature of investments held in the portfolio. Investors choose balanced or hybrid funds depending on their retirement plans. For instance, a retired person would choose a conservative fund, because the investor cannot afford to risk their retirement money.

Target funds are expensive and may also be more aggressive or volatile than you may want. If you want to invest in a target fund, check out a low-cost provider like Vanguard. Also, I want to remind you that you can create an asset allocation based on your risk tolerance and objectives instead of paying target fund fees and reducing your return on your investment. Keep in mind to diversify through low-cost index funds. For example, if you are in your eighties, the general rule of thumb is to have 40 percent of your portfolio invested in bonds, but if you are in your thirties, be invested 100 percent in equities.

Index funds can vary by sector, location, and size. It is not recommended to invest in just one market, e.g., emerging markets. It is prudent to invest in a well-diversified portfolio which may include 30 percent US, 30 percent Europe, 20 percent Asia/Pacific, and 20 percent in emerging markets.

Alternative funds are multifaceted investments that include hedge funds, managed futures, commodities, socially responsible funds, and real estate funds. Before investing in these funds, investors should do extensive research to find out the risk and the returns expected in each of these funds. Alternative funds are more complex than the conventional mutual fund strategies. Alternative funds can achieve higher returns, but they also have higher risks. Also, they require higher minimum investments and a longer maturity date.

In summary, there are many investment choice alternatives, but you must select those investments that will meet your desired financial objective, risk appetite, and time frame.

5

INVESTMENT PORTFOLIO AND CAPITAL APPRECIATION

"Don't wish it was easier, wish you were better. Don't wish for less problems, wish for more skills. Don't wish for less challenge, wish for more wisdom."

— JIM ROHN

An investment portfolio may be composed of stocks, bonds, and cash. Your investment strategy will guide your day-to-day decisions on investing, both short- and long-term. Portfolio planning considers the investor's financial goals and risk tolerance and time frame among other factors. When creating your investment portfolio, you must also take into consideration asset allocation. Asset allocation is more than diversification; you need to determine, based on your financial goals, risk tolerance, and stage of life, what percentage of your portfolio you want to invest in the different investment classes such as stocks, bonds, commodities, real estate, etcetera. Your asset allocation is your long-term strategy for diversified investing. Your portfolio strategy based on your overall investment objectives guides your investment choices and takes care of your future needs by achieving capital appreciation, namely an increase in the price or value of your assets. Your portfolio strategy takes into consideration not only your investment goals but also your liquidity needs, risk tolerance, time horizon, and minimization of your tax burden.

For example, a single woman in her thirties can invest in an aggressive fund that yields capital appreciation. In any case, on the off chance that you are a couple in your forties with youngsters moving toward college age, you can't risk your cash in aggressive stocks that might suffer losses exactly when the cash is required to pay for your children's college education. Be that as it may, with retirement far later on, you may also need a portion of your cash in an aggressive fund while most is invested in conservative choices. The same couple, when they reach retirement age, may invest most of their money in income-producing investments to add to their month-to-month retirement income. Therefore, your portfolio allocation needs to be based on your current and future financial needs and objectives.

Risk tolerance is the degree of uncertainty that an investor can handle. For instance, risk-averse investors like to minimize the possibility of a financial loss and, therefore, invest in lower risk investments such as government bonds. The lower the risk, the lower the rates of return. The higher the risk, the higher the rates of return on investment. Are you risk-tolerant or risk-averse? The appropriate response is critical to your portfolio plan, and it might change after some time. An individual investor can build a portfolio plan alone or with the assistance of an experienced fiduciary. On the off chance that you are a conservative investor, your portfolio will have both capital appreciation and income. Conservative portfolios, as a rule, invest in conservative allocation of funds, hold a smaller amount of equities than moderate-allocation portfolios, and have much lower risk than the aggressive fund portfolio.

A solid financial plan incorporates a mission statement, a dynamic structure, investment objectives and strategy, risk profile, and a portfolio-monitoring procedure. The expression "portfolio investments" covers a wide scope of asset classes including bonds, government securities, corporate securities, real estate investment trusts (REITs), common stocks, exchange-traded funds (ETFs), and certificates of deposit. Portfolio investments can likewise hold investments such as warrants, derivatives, and futures as well as other tangible investments such as real estate, commodities, art, etcetera.

On a bigger scope, mutual funds and large institutional investors are in the business of making portfolio investments which may include large infrastructure investments like bridges and expressways.

Investors saving for retirement often invest in a diversified portfolio and low-cost investments such as index funds. Index funds have become popular in individual retirement accounts and 401(k) accounts. Investors who enjoy a more hands-on approach like to manage their portfolio allocations by including selected stocks and bonds and adding additional investments such as real estate and private equity. The capital appreciation on an investment is the increase in value of the investment. To know what the capital appreciation of an investment is, take away the initial investment from the current value. For instance, say you purchased 100 shares of stock for $75 per share and they are currently worth $79 each. Taking away the underlying cost of $75-per-share from the current value of $79-per-share gives you a capital appreciation of $4-per-share. To determine the total capital appreciation, multiply the $4-per-share increment by 100 shares, resulting in a total capital appreciation of $400. Of course, only when you sell the stock will you realize such gain.

If the stock market were to go down and the price of your shares were to come down to $70 per share, you will have a $500 loss on paper. Due to the volatility in the stock market, the Internal Revenue Service (IRS) only charges you taxes when you sell your investment and realize a gain. For instance, say you own stock that has appreciated in value by $400. You do not owe any taxes until you sell the stock and realize the gain. You will have to pay taxes the year that you sold the stock. Capital appreciation does not include dividends, which are payments made by the company to the shareholders, and you also pay taxes on dividends received from the investment. For instance, say you purchased a stock for $75, it has appreciated to $79, and it has $5 in dividends. While the capital appreciation is just $4, the overall return is $9, and you must pay taxes on the $9.

The tax rate that you pay on the capital appreciation when you sell the investment depends upon how long you held it. In the event that you owned the stock for a year or less, you pay taxes on ordinary income. If you owned it for more than a year, you pay tax based on long-term capital gain rates. The 2019 to 2020 Long-Term Capital Gains charge rates are 0, 15, or 20 percent, depending upon your taxable income and filing status.

Real estate investors are permitted to take depreciation deductions depending on the wear and tear of the property. Those depreciation deductions give you a tax reduction now, but they also reduce your tax basis. For instance, if you purchase a building for $800,000 and you are allowed to claim $40,000 in depreciation, then when you sell it, your tax basis would be $760,000. Paying as little as possible on capital gains taxes is significant. There are various techniques you can use to bring down your tax bill. Timing the sale of your appreciated assets is the best and least-demanding approach to deal with your capital gains taxes. Remember that paper gains are not taxable. You'll only pay taxes when you sell those investments and it is always up to you when you sell them.

Ensuring that you hold onto winning investments long enough to get the lower capital gains tax rate is a popular tax strategy. That doesn't mean it always works; sometimes an investment makes money shortly after you purchase it, and holding it for the whole year may not work because the investment may also decrease in value. However, if you are close to the one-year mark, holding onto the investment may make a difference between a large and a much smaller tax bill. Investors often take capital losses to offset any capital gains that they may have in their portfolio. This tax strategy is often done toward the end of the year as people begin to plan to file their tax returns for the year. It is important to remember that you do not pay taxes when selling investments inside a qualified retirement account such as an Individual Retirement Account (IRA) or 401(k).

RETIREMENT PLANS

There are many kinds of retirement plans, including IRAs, Roth IRAs, 401(k) plans, 403(b) plans, simple IRA plans (savings incentive match plans for employees), SEP plans (simplified employee pension), SARSEP plans (salary reduction simplified employee pension), payroll deduction IRAs, profit-sharing plans, defined benefit plans, money purchase plans, employee stock ownership plans (ESOPs), governmental plans, and 457 plans. For assistance to select the right retirement plan for you, visit this link: https://www.irs.gov/pub/irs-tege/savings_retirement.pdf.

401(K) VERSUS IRA

The 401(k) retirement plan started in 1984 and gave employees the opportunity to participate in the stock market and save on taxes by making tax-deductible contributions from their paychecks. The greatest distinction between the two most well-known kinds of retirement accounts, 401(k) and IRA, is that 401(k) plans are set up by employers and IRAs are individual retirement accounts. With 401(k) accounts, contributions are made on a pre-tax basis.

Contributions to IRA accounts are made post-tax income; however, deductions are available for these contributions. With both IRA and 401(k) plans, investments grow on a tax-deferred basis; however, at withdrawal, taxes are due at the then-current tax rate. There are different contribution limits and tax considerations for both retirement accounts. Most plans offer a spread of mutual funds composed of stocks, bonds, and money market investments, and it is important for you to know that these mutual funds have many different fees and costs between the underlying investments and the plan administration, which reduce the overall investment returns. For more information about these retirement plans, visit the following link: https://www.diffen.com/difference/401k-vs-IRA.

A Roth IRA is an IRA used for retirement savings. The Roth IRA has no withdrawal requirements and tax-exempt qualified withdrawals after age fifty-nine-and-a-half. To qualify for a Roth IRA, you must have earned income and meet adjusted gross income prerequisites. You can start taking tax-exempt withdrawals after fifty-nine-and-a-half and keep making contributions after age seventy-and-a-half. The yearly contribution limit for 2019 and 2020 is $6,000, or $7,000 in the case that you are age fifty or older. On the off chance that you own a business, you can start a SEP-IRA. An SEP plan permits employers to add to conventional IRAs (SEP-IRAs) set up for employees. A business of any size, even independently employed, can set up a SEP. For detailed information about retirement plans, go to this link: https://www.irs.gov/retirement-plans/plan-sponsor/types-of-retirement-plans.

6

INVESTING IN AGGRESSIVE STOCKS WITH HIGH GROWTH OR BONDS WITH HIGH YIELD POTENTIAL

"October. This is one of the peculiarly dangerous months to speculate in stocks in. The others are July, January, September, April, November, May, March, June, December, August and February."

— MARK TWAIN

When purchasing stocks, bonds, or any other investment alternatives, take care not to time the stock market because you can't predict it; even the best in the world can't do it year after year. Instead, diversify across time and implement a dollar-cost average investment strategy to diversify across asset classes and across markets. Also, it is advisable to rebalance your portfolio at least once a year to make sure that your asset allocations are still in the correct proportion based on your desired outcome.

In any case, how would you really begin? You can manage an investment portfolio by opening an online brokerage account at E-trade (https://us.etrade.com) or at Schwab (https://www.schwab.com/), which is the fastest and most affordable way to purchase stocks, bonds, index funds, and an assortment of different investments.

To start your investment process, you can choose amongst two investment types: mutual funds or exchange traded funds versus individual stocks. When you invest in an equity fund, you own a small piece of each of the companies in the fund. If you decide to invest in a specific company, you can purchase shares; notwithstanding, in the event that you are simply beginning to invest into stocks, an equity fund will give you a diversified investment and will minimize your risk of losing money. Investing in individual stocks is risky and the amount of money that you need to buy a stock depends on the market value of the specific stock. If you are beginning to invest in the stock market, it is best to buy an S&P 500 index fund. However, if you think that an individual stock has long-term potential, individual stocks could be a good investment for your portfolio, but you must remember to diversify your portfolio. Portfolio diversification means that an investor decides to hold in her investment portfolio various types of securities and investments from different issuers and industries and invests in assets that are not significantly correlated with one another. Portfolio diversification is key, according to Warren Buffett. Warren is considered one of the most successful investors in the world and has a net worth of US$69.7 billion in 2020, making him the fourth-wealthiest person in the world. In the event that individual stocks or bonds appeal to you, figuring out how to research these investments is essential to augment your overall return on your investments. Therefore, it would be a good idea to subscribe to a research company such as the Standard & Poor's, which offers access to individual company financial reports on a subscription basis. A subscription to Morningstar gets you access to reports on 1,800 companies. Their analysts favor companies with a defensible advantage whose stocks sell at a discount to a firm's true worth, which they estimate by forecasting future cash flows. The answer to how to invest really comes down to two things: the time horizon for your goals and how much risk you are willing to take.

WHAT IS YOUR TIME HORIZON?

If you are investing for a faraway objective such as your retirement, you ought to invest basically in stocks. Investing in stocks will permit your money to grow and outpace inflation. As your objective draws nearer, you can gradually begin to dial back your stock allocation and include more bonds, which are safer investments.

WHAT IS YOUR RISK TOLERANCE?

The stock market fluctuates up and down, so if you are a conservative investor, it is best if your portfolio has a smaller allocation of volatile stocks. You may want to consider investing in a mutual fund such as the S&P 500 which will provide you with diversification and minimize your overall risk. However, if your risk tolerance is high and you are a young investor, you have time to play the stock market and you can win or lose depending on the stock that you hold in your portfolio. Emotion is not your friend when trading stocks. Prior to trading, you must know when to buy and when to sell to achieve your desired outcome. That's how Warren Buffett has made big money in the past, from the bear market of 1974 to the financial crisis of 2008. "Be fearful when others are greedy," he famously advised, "and... be greedy only when others are fearful."

The big questions are not "When will the economy recover?" or "Where will the market go next?" The questions to consider include:

1. How can I get the highest return with the least amount of risk?
2. How can I protect profits and principal?
3. What can I do to make sure that my investment portfolio will be worth more in the future?

Success in investing starts by selecting the right stock, buying at the lowest price, minimizing expenses, and knowing your exit strategy. There are many research companies that can help you with the above questions. My favorite is the Oxford Club's website: https://oxfordclub.com/.

BONDS

Bonds are one of the most significant investments accessible for the individuals who have an income investment portfolio and plan to live off the income produced by their bond and fixed income portfolio. There is a wide range of fixed investment choices accessible to you, including municipal, commercial, savings, and treasury bonds. You need to know which of these bonds are the best investment for you based on your overall financial objectives. There are a number of bonds where you can invest, and many more ways you can hold these bonds. Benjamin Graham, known as "the father of value investing" and a mentor to Warren Buffet, believes that a conservative investor should never have less than 25 percent of their portfolio in bonds. Municipal bonds are excluded from certain state taxes under certain investment opportunities. If you are in a middle- to high-income tax bracket, you should hold municipal bonds in your portfolio. Also, by investing in municipal bonds, you could be investing in your nearby schools, hospitals, and municipalities in your community and also be enjoying a good return on your money. To learn more about municipal, corporate, agency, and government bond offerings, visit the link below:

https://www.thebondcenter.com/hennionandwalsh/?gclid=EAIaIQobChMI06OFteuJ6gIVA4TICh2x3wdOEAAYASAAEgIaMvD_BwE.

7

ALTERNATIVE INVESTMENTS FOR YOUR PORTFOLIO

"What's worth doing is worth doing for money."

— GORDON GEKKO

Let's start by defining alternative asset investments. These range from real estate and precious metals to more speculative investments such as hard money loans and cryptocurrencies. Bitcoin has been on a wild ride since its origin, but this hasn't halted speculators' conviction that cryptos are a developing business sector. If you have a self-directed IRA, you can invest your money in alternative assets such as real estate.

There are two primary reasons to invest in alternative assets – diversity and volatility. Even though, over time, the stock market has yielded a reasonably good return, the stock market is unpredictable.

Therefore, every investment expert will concur that you ought to have a diversified portfolio and alternative asset investments are a good alternative. You can consider protecting your assets against inflation by buying precious metals, earning passive income from real estate investments, or earning money for making hard money loans. All these can diversify your portfolio, but you should only have up to 10 percent of your funds in alternative investments. Closed-end funds are a lesser-known kind of mutual fund. When investing in closed-end funds, investors know that their funds will not be available for seven to ten years. Private equity fund partners are the general partners, and investors are the limited partners. The limited partnership agreement details the amount of risk that each party takes along with the time duration of the fund. Venture capital investment (VC) is a type of private equity financing that is given by investment firms or funds to finance the operations of new companies that have been deemed to have high potential growth. The VCs invest in these new companies in exchange for a percentage of the company ownership and expect to obtain high returns. It should be noted that venture capital investment is highly risky and not advisable for a beginner investor.

Hedge funds are alternative investments that trade with highly complex trading strategies such as short selling, leverage, and derivatives to obtain a higher return for their investors. Hedge funds are only accessible to accredited investors because they require less Securities and Exchange Commission (SEC) regulation than other funds. Examples of accredited investors include a bank, an investment company registered under the Investment Company Act of 1940, and a small business investment company registered under the Small Business Investment Company Act of 1958.

Commodities are natural resources that originate from the earth. A few examples of commodities include wheat, cattle, soybeans, corn, oranges, precious metals, coal, cotton, and oil. Investors focus on raw materials for their manufactured products that consumers end up buying. Some of the ways to invest in commodities include investing directly in the commodity, using commodity future contracts, and buying shares in the companies that produce commodities. The best commodities in which to invest directly are those commodities where logistics are easier to handle, such as gold and silver.

Real estate as an alternative investment requires industry knowledge, a specific network, and accredited investment status. The return to investors could prove greater than the return from average securities. Investors could invest in long-term rental properties, short-term house flipping, or real estate investment trusts. The latter investment is easiest to manage since the long-term rental properties and the short-term house flipping require the investor's time and additional capital input to manage and improve these properties. A real estate investment trust (REIT) invests in real estate that generates income. Most REITs have practical experience in a particular real estate sector, centering their time, vitality, and financing on that specific segment of the real estate industry. Be that as it may, diversified REITs frequently hold various kinds of properties in their portfolios, including apartment complexes, high-rises, commercial buildings, retail centers, self-storages, warehouses, and distribution centers. One advantage of REITs for investors is that REITs give the chance to own a portion of the real estate that generates dividend-based income. The main business objective of REITs is to lease space and collect rents on the investment properties and distribute that income as dividends to investors.

Equity REITs are the most widely recognized REITs. The equity REITs purchase, own, and oversee income-producing real estate. Their income comes basically through rents and not from the reselling of the portfolio properties.

Mortgage REITs lend money to real estate owners and operators. The loaning might be either directly through home loans and advances or indirectly through the acquisition of mortgage-backed securities.

Hybrid REITs hold both physical rental property

and mortgage loans in their portfolio. See below a chart describing both the various types of REITs and the nature of their holdings.

Type of REIT	Holdings
Equity	Own and operate income-producing real estate
Mortgage	Provide mortgages on real property
Hybrid	Own properties and make mortgages
Publicly Traded	Listing on a national exchange
Public Non-traded	Registered with the SEC but not publicly traded
Private	Work only as private placement investments

Publicly traded REITs offer shares that list on a national securities exchange, where they are bought and sold by individual investors. They are regulated by the US Securities and Exchange Commission (SEC).

Public non-traded REITs likewise are registered with the SEC but don't trade on national securities exchanges. Thus, the non-traded REITs are less liquid than REITs that are traded on the open market, but non-traded REITs are not subject to daily market fluctuations. **Private REITs** are not registered with the SEC and don't trade in the stock markets, therefore, there is little to no public or independent performance data that investors can use to track their investments.

REITs can have a significant influence on an investment portfolio. Similarly, as with all investments, they have their advantages and disadvantages. REITs are easy to buy and sell as most trade in the public exchanges. This attractive component mitigates a portion of the downsides of real estate. Often, real estate lacks transparency and the property can take time to buy and/or sell depending on tax considerations, zoning, and market conditions.

REITs are regulated by the SEC and must file annual audited financial statements. REITs don't offer much capital appreciation. They must pay out to the investors 90 percent of their income, and the remaining 10 percent can be reinvested to buy new property. The dividends received from REITs are taxed as ordinary income, and REITs, like most investments, do not guarantee a profit or insure against losses. Furthermore, REITs have high management and transaction fees; however, they do offer liquidity, diversification, transparency, dividends, and risk-adjusted returns. There are around 225 publicly traded REITs in the US, which implies you will have some research to do before choosing which REIT will work best for your portfolio. For more data about how to invest in REITs, go to www.reit.com.

8

INVESTING IN REAL ESTATE

"Carpe per diem – seize the check."

— ROBIN WILLIAMS

The homeownership rate in the United States was 64.2 percent in 2018. This rate differs contingent upon the demographics of households, such as ethnicity, race, type of household, and location. For some Americans, owning a home is a fundamental piece of the American dream that gives various monetary advantages including the capacity to gather wealth and access credit by building home equity. If you have a mortgage on your property, you may be surprised to see your thirty-year mortgage being paid off in fifteen years if you were to prepay your next month's principal. If you are financially able to do so, next time you write your monthly mortgage check, write a second check for the principal-only portion of your next month's payment.

Buying real estate is a popular way to invest and build equity. There are various ways of investing in real estate to build equity and create cash flow. Owning investment properties is a good method to make extra income while building home equity. Also, when you decide to sell, you could earn additional profit depending on the type of property that you buy and how you manage it. When you buy a property for investment, location is important because it will affect its appreciation and its resale value. Another way to build equity and create cash flow is flipping a property, which means you purchase it, make updates and improvements, and then sell it within a short period of time. If you sell the property within a year, you will pay ordinary income tax on the profit. However, when you sell an investment property after owning it for at least a year, you'll pay capital gains tax on the profit.

The single greatest asset that many individuals have is their home, and they may realize capital gains on the sale of their home. According to the current tax laws, if you are a homeowner, you are allowed to exclude up to $250,000 of your gain if you are single, and $500,000 if you are married filing jointly, provided that you owned and use the home as your primary residence for at least two years in the five-year period before the sale, and that you have not excluded the gain from another home sale in the two-year period before the sale.

Keep in mind that if you sell your property within a year, you will pay short-term capital gains taxes which are significantly higher than the long-term capital gains taxes, typically 10 to 20 percent higher. Therefore, to minimize capital gains taxes, and if you want to sell your property, sell after owning it for more than one year. It should also be noted that people in the lowest tax bracket usually do not have to pay any tax on long-term capital gains.

Your capital losses can offset your capital gains. For instance, if you sell an investment property for less than its cost basis, you have a capital loss that can offset your capital gains. Savvy investors defer paying capital gains taxes by taking advantage of Section 1031 of the IRS code 1031 exchange. The aforementioned is an important rule to know because you can legally minimize and/or defer paying capital gains taxes.

The IRS code's Section 1031 makes it feasible for an investor to defer paying capital gains taxes on an investment property upon its sale – as long as another "like kind" property is purchased with the profit from the sale of the investment property. A delayed exchange is the most common exchange type because the exchanger gets a lot of time to find the property and close it. For example, if an investor were to sell a property and receive $1,000,000 in net proceeds, the investor will have to pay taxes on the gain; however, by utilizing a 1031 exchange, the investor may defer paying taxes and preserve all the profit from the sale of the property. The proceeds from the sale of the investment property are kept by a third party known as a qualified intermediary (QI). A three-party exchange is needed for a taxpayer to carry out the "like kind" exchange, which is a powerful tax-deferment strategy used by successful investors. Any investment property other than your primary residence qualifies for an exchange.

In summary, real estate is a good alternative investment for your portfolio, especially considering all the tax incentives associated with owning investment property and/or the tax advantages of owning a home. Of course, keep in mind that diversification is one of the golden rules of your investment portfolio.

9

THERE ARE MANY INVESTMENT ALTERNATIVES WHEN PLANNING FOR RETIREMENT

"Money isn't the most important thing in life, but it's reasonably close to oxygen on the 'gotta have it' scale."

— ZIG ZIGLAR

Before you start getting ready for retirement, you must consider how much cash you need. You should make a few assumptions with respect to the length of your retirement years, make a reasonable budget, and plan for unforeseeable circumstances such as, for example, sickness. In other words, begin with an end in mind. Consider saving 15 percent of your pre-tax salary each year (including any employer contribution). If you are starting later in life, you may want to save even more depending on your overall financial situation. If you are eligible for Social Security benefits, you can start collecting benefits as early as age sixty-two – but that may not be the right strategy for you.

The median age when an American retires is sixty-two. But every situation is unique. Want to retire to a less expensive city? Work part-time in retirement? When building your plan, you can explore a variety of scenarios. In retirement, some expenses like a mortgage or childcare might decrease, but health care expenses will likely rise. An average sixty-five-year-old couple can expect to pay $288,400 over the course of retirement in Medicare premiums alone.

If you don't have a 401(k) at work, or even if you've contributed enough to get the maximum employer match, it is a good idea to open an individual retirement account (IRA) to save more money for your retirement. Both 401(k)s and IRAs have tax benefits. However, IRAs are set up and kept up by you, and 401(k)s are maintained by your employer. With an IRA, you ordinarily get a wide selection of investments, frequently significantly more than in a 401(k). Investors achieve portfolio diversification through asset allocation by investing in stocks, bonds, cash, etcetera in order to minimize portfolio risk. Lower risk investments have lower risk but also lower returns. Investors seeking higher returns have to take more risk. If you are retirement age or need to retire in less than five years, it is best to have in your portfolio lower-risk investments because you will not have the time to recover before having to have access to the money.

A conservative asset allocation is designed to protect the value of the portfolio by investing in low-risk investments such as cash or bonds since the time horizon is less than five years. A moderate asset allocation seeks growth with moderate risk and invests in a diversified stock portfolio since the funds will not be needed for at least seven years and the investor will have time to recover from potential losses. An aggressive portfolio holds riskier investments with the goal to achieve higher returns. Here, I am reminded of one of my favorite Warren Buffett quotes: "Rule number one: never lose money. Rule number two: never forget rule number one."

If you work as a teacher, school administrator, professor, government employee, nurse, doctor, or librarian, you will enjoy a 403(b) retirement plan, which is a retirement account for certain employees of public schools and tax-exempt organizations. Religious ministers may also participate in these plans. The 403(b) resembles the 401(k), but the 403(b) plan serves employees of public schools and tax-exempt organizations rather than private-sector workers.

The 403(b) plan and the 401(k) plan have similar advantages, and both have the same contribution limits of $19,500 in 2020.

Similarly, as with a 401(k), funds withdrawn

from a 403(b) plan before age fifty-nine-and-a-half are subject to a 10 percent tax penalty. However, you may avoid the penalty if you leave your employer at age fifty-five or older or need qualified medical care. A 403(b) offers a smaller selection of investments than a 401(k) plan because the 401(k) plan is administered by mutual fund companies. The 403(b) plans offer fixed annuities and variable annuities with mutual funds options. It should be noted that these plans do not offer the opportunity to invest in stocks and riskier investment alternatives. Variable annuities are long-term investment products intended for retirement purposes and are subject to market fluctuation, investment risk, and possible loss of principal. Variable annuities contain both investment and insurance components but have high expense fees and charges, including mortality cost.

A 457(b) retirement plan is a non-qualified tax-deferred compensation plan similar to qualified plans such as the 401(k) and 403(b). The 457(b) plan is offered by a state or local government. The 457(b) retirement plan may be available as an additional voluntary retirement savings vehicle for state or local government or tax-exempt organization employers also offering a public employees' pension system. Or they can be offered as a supplemental retirement option for those state or local government or tax-exempt organization employers offering a 401(k) or 403(b) plan. The 457(b) plans rarely provide an employer-matching contribution, and there is no federal 10 percent premature distribution penalty imposed on withdrawals when separating from service.

To minimize your expenses, before investing, evaluate the fees and expenses of the investment options available in the 457(b), 403(b), and 401(k) plans you are considering. Each plan chooses which investment alternatives to offer eligible employees, so fund choices and associated fees and expenses vary. Talk with a fiduciary advisor about the many investment alternatives when planning for retirement and how best to protect your income as part of your retirement strategy.

10

MANAGING YOUR RETIREMENT ACCOUNT, ANNUITIES, AND LONG-TERM CARE

"If you're given a choice between money and sex appeal, take the money. As you get older, the money will become your sex appeal."

— KATHERINE HEPBURN

In Chapters 7, 8, and 9, you have reviewed various investment alternatives to fund your retirement account, have learned to invest consistently on a monthly basis, and have selected investment alternatives depending on your time horizon and risk tolerance. Now I will turn my attention to how best to make your money last longer through annuities and long-term care insurance.

Annuities allow you to grow your future income while offering alternatives to help ensure against market downturns, to provide protected monthly income for life, to ensure you a comfortable retirement, and/or for passing on the benefit to your family. There are various kinds of annuities, namely **fixed annuity, variable annuity,** and **indexed annuity**. Fixed annuity has the lowest risk and the most predictability. Variable annuity has risks and potentially higher returns. Indexed Annuity has the characteristics of both fixed and variable annuities. However, it should be noted that annuities have high fees and they are intended for long-term investment.

Long-term care: despite the fact that such huge numbers of individuals appear to be worried about long-term care costs and their effect on future retirement success, a small percentage of people buy protection to cover this risk. In contrast to conventional medical coverage, long-term care protection is intended to cover custodial care. Long-term care protection strategies repay policyholders for everyday custodial care to help them with activities of day-by-day living, for example, washing, dressing, or eating. The cost of long-term care is based on the following factors:

- How old you are when you buy the policy
- The maximum amount that a policy will pay per day
- The maximum number of days (years) that a policy will pay
- The maximum amount per day times the

number of days (to determine the lifetime maximum amount that the policy will pay)
- Any optional benefits you choose, such as benefits that increase with inflation

If you are in poor health, you will not qualify for long-term care insurance since it requires medical underwriting. Although expensive, sometimes you might have the option to purchase a limited amount of coverage. Most policies will pay the costs of your long-term care for two to five years while a few policies will pay for as long as you live. Some public programs, including Medicare and Medicaid, may help pay for some long-term care services. Be that as it may, each program has explicit rules about what services are covered, how long you can receive benefits and get advantages, and the amount you need to pay out-of-pocket. Medicare pays for health care of people age sixty-five and older. Medicare covers medically necessary care such as doctor's visits, drugs, and hospital stays. Medicare doesn't pay for custodial services such as bathing.

Generally, you are eligible for Medicare (the initial enrollment period for Part C and Part D) when you turn sixty-five. However, you qualify to receive Medicare under sixty-five years old if you are disabled. Each year, you can make changes to your Medicare Advantage or Medicare prescription drug coverage for the following year. There are two separate enrollment periods each year. You can generally join one of these Medicare Advantage plans:

- Health Maintenance Organization (HMO)
- Preferred Provider Organization (PPO)
- Private Fee-for-Service (PFFS)
- Medical Savings Account (MSA) Plan

Eligibility and Medicare plans are complex. For detailed information about Medicare benefits, go to the following website: www.medicare.gov.

If you're over sixty-five (or turning sixty-five in the next three months) and not already getting benefits from Social Security, you need to sign up to get Medicare Part A (Hospital Insurance) and Part B (Medical Insurance). You will not get Medicare automatically.

Sign up for Medicare online or contact Social Security. Social Security will review your records to see if you qualify for Medicare: https://www.ssa.-gov/benefits/medicare/.

Medicaid is a joint federal and state government program that helps individuals with low income pay for some or the entirety of their health care bills including long-term care services in nursing homes. In contrast to Medicare, Medicaid pays for custodial care in nursing homes and at home. To be qualified for Medicaid you should meet certain requirements, including having income that doesn't surpass the levels utilized by your state. For detailed information on Medicaid eligibility, go to: https://www.hhs.-gov/answers/medicare-and-medicaid/who-is-eligi-ble-for-medicaid/index.html.

In summary, this chapter covering annuities, long-term care, Medicare, and Medicaid are not applicable to a younger reader, but it is important to know how best to plan to maximize your benefits at the appropriate time.

11

ADVANTAGES AND DISADVANTAGES OF LIFE INSURANCE

"Money is something you have to make in case you don't die."

— MAX ASNAS

The reason for life insurance is to give financial protection to surviving dependents after the demise of an insured person. There are basically two types of life insurance policies: whole life and term insurance.

Whole life insurance coverage is more costly than term life coverage, but the payout that the beneficiary receives after the insured dies is tax-free. You can renew your term insurance policy when it expires but the premiums will be higher, or you can convert your term policy to a permanent life insurance policy at the end of the term. Term insurance is a great option when you have kids or while you are paying a mortgage. You can also customize a whole life insurance policy with riders depending on your overall insurance needs. Such riders can include term conversion, disability income, long-term care, critical illness, waiver of premium, or unemployment protection. For example, for an additional charge, you can customize your whole life insurance to include a long-term care rider. Term life insurance is available in ten-year, fifteen-year, twenty-year, or thirty-year terms, and is renewable annually. A key step in buying insurance protection is picking your beneficiary. Your beneficiary can be one person, for instance your husband or your wife, or two or more people such as your children. By designating your beneficiaries, you have the final say over who receives your death benefits; therefore, as your life changes, it is important to review your life insurance policies to make sure that you still have the right beneficiary designations in your insurance policies.

Some of the questions you will need to consider are: Who will require additional cash when you pass on? Are there individuals who rely upon you for money? Are there individuals who will bear certain costs at your passing? Who receives the funds if none of your beneficiaries survive you? Should the funds pass to your estate or your trust? With most insurance policies, you can change your beneficiaries at any time. You don't need to figure it all out by yourself. Contact your fiduciary advisor today to examine your specific insurance needs.

Universal life insurance provides permanent life insurance protection with no need to renew the policy with higher premiums, and the death benefit paid to your beneficiaries is tax-free. With some universal life insurance policies, you can also build cash value and have access to cash while you are still alive, and the cash value that you withdraw from the policy is also tax-free. A special blend of universal life insurance and long-term care insurance coverage can provide you with death benefits to your beneficiaries as well as with cash value to help with long-term care custodial expenses. It should be noted that the major advantage of the universal life policy is its flexibility in regard to frequency of payments and flexible death benefits.

The advantages of life insurance are greater than its disadvantages. For instance, life insurance can be used for many functions in estate planning, including the following:

1. Term or whole life insurance can be purchased on an individual to provide funds for the surviving spouse or children when death occurs.
2. Whole life insurance can be purchased to provide income to the parents at retirement. This can occur by converting

the policy to an annuity or by withdrawing the cash value.

3. Life insurance can provide dollars that can be passed on as an inheritance.
4. Life insurance can be used to provide funds for the payment of estate taxes, estate settlement costs, or debt obligations of the deceased.
5. Life insurance can provide income at the time of the parent's death for the buyout of land, machinery, or operating assets from other heirs, if the parents have distributed their farm assets equally among all their children.
6. Farming or business partners often buy insurance on each other. This process provides funds for buying out the deceased partner's assets if a premature death occurs. This enables the living partner to keep the farm or business intact.
7. Life insurance can be used to create or enhance an estate. It can be an estate building plan providing money to heirs.
8. There are some life insurance choices that enable people to draw on the death benefit to cover long-term health care costs.

In summary, work with your fiduciary advisor to evaluate your life insurance as family, estate, and business needs change throughout your lifetime. Life insurance plays an important role in your estate planning. Depending on your overall financial needs, you can determine if term or whole life insurance plans are best suited for your needs. To learn more about life insurance and to identify the best insurance company for your needs, visit the following link: https://www.nerdwallet.com/blog/insurance/best-life-insurance-companies/.

12

IMPLEMENTING A COMPREHENSIVE FINANCIAL PLAN

"Create the highest, grandest vision possible for your life, because you become what you believe."

— OPRAH WINFREY

To implement a comprehensive financial plan, you first need to create a vision for your life. A few years ago, through my daily meditation, I learned to focus on and clarify twelve areas of my life. Daily meditation is important because it enables you to become aware of how you show up in the world and how you perceive reality. You are in a unique position to create your own reality based on your vision for your life. To create your life vision, I encourage you to consider and evaluate not only your financial well-being but also the following areas of your life.

HEALTH AND FITNESS

In terms of your health and fitness goals, you should identify precisely what you need, why you need it, and what you have to do to get it. While it is difficult to keep away from all worry throughout everyday life, limiting stressors and dealing with the manner in which you react to pressure can have significant advantages. You may want to take a break from an unpleasant circumstance by tuning in to quieting music and relaxation. Often times, doing a breathing exercise or even taking a full breath can help. Daily exercise is known to be advantageous for diminishing pressure. While all types of activity appear to work, my favorite relaxing exercises include yoga and Tai Chi. Increasingly more research shows that getting enough sleep, eating healthy, and daily exercise can reduce stress.

INTELLECTUAL

Intellectual wellness is the capacity to be available to new thoughts, to think critically, to learn new skills, to make potential for sharing with other people, and to use it for the improvement of your community. Scholarly activity enhances intellectual wellness just as learning new and exciting things does. A decent method to expand your scholarly health is to peruse for no particular reason. Reading, particularly something you appreciate, can improve your insight by extending your psyche to consider things you normally don't consider. Improve your skills in studying and learning. Also, learning new things about the way your mind processes information can be a vital tool for helping you succeed.

Write down your thoughts or journal frequently. Taking the time to do this can help those who struggle with expressing their feelings or, in general, can help anyone who is trying to make sense of what they are feeling inside. Being able to identify your feelings and understanding yourself and your actions more increases intellectual wellness by exposing your mind to deeper thinking.

EMOTIONAL

It is important to explore the nature of your emotions in order to make your feelings and emotions work for you as opposed to living in response mode. Don't hesitate to share your emotions and ideas with your family and dear companions. Emotional intelligence is our capacity to comprehend and intelligently use our various feelings and emotions in our life. It's less about controlling your feelings, which suggests that you limit, stifle, or deny them; rather, it's about dealing with your feelings and emotions, which includes being adaptable with your reasoning, conduct, and reactions and being open to sharing your pleasant and unpleasant feelings and emotions with the people around you.

You can learn to better manage your emotional intelligence skills at any age or phase of life. What's more, emotional intelligence leads to better mental and physical well-being and, generally speaking, life fulfillment. Probably the most straightforward approach to improving your emotional intelligence is to distinguish your sources of stress to minimize them. Some stress-help measures include practicing yoga, deep breathing, meditation, or going for a run. These measures are unique to each individual, so find out what is your best way to minimize stress in your life. For instance, one of my stress minimizers is a deep tissue massage.

CHARACTER

This is one of the most important categories that influences each aspect of your life. During this powerful internal exploration, you will discover the individual that you need to become to accomplish the life you want. You will figure out how to deliberately pick the character traits you need to build into your life and create a strategy to achieve them. A person's character is who they truly are. Abraham Lincoln once said, "Character is like a tree and reputation like its shadow. The shadow is what we think of it; the tree is the real thing." My reputation is what others think of me, which could possibly be valid, however, my character is who I truly am. Your character is your genuine self, as in, you can't separate what you do from what your identity is. To create character, start by featuring your most significant values. At that point, search for approaches to maintain those values consistently, even in immaterial circumstances. Additionally, take a look at the companions and colleagues who you invest the most energy with. Encircle yourself with individuals you appreciate to additionally move you to reinforce your character.

SPIRITUAL

According to Dr. Deepak Chopra, "Everyday life is impossible without holding your own set of beliefs." The vast majority of people are guided by faith in the work they do, their religion, commitment to their family, and a wide range of values they hold dear. During your reflective journey into your spirituality, examine your values and beliefs, the world and your place in it. Some of the ways you can boost your spiritual growth include reading spiritual and uplifting books and magazines and applying what you learn to your everyday life, meditating each day for at least fifteen minutes, thinking positively by opening the door to positive thoughts/ideas and closing the door to negative ones, understanding that you are a spirit with a physical body and not the other way around, celebrating the moments that make you feel present and alive, developing patience and tolerance for others, and being grateful to the Universe for the things you have been given, whether it's a beautiful fall day or an afternoon by the water.

LOVE RELATIONSHIPS

Establish clarity about what you truly need in this aspect of your life and recognize what steps you can take to make and sustain a phenomenal love relationship. What might your optimal love relationship be? Is trust one of the most significant values for you in a relationship? In the event that you don't trust the individual you are with, then it is probably not a sound, stable relationship and you in all likelihood feel uncertain about it. What about respect? No measure of love merits surrendering who you are and the respect you deserve as a person. Partners must be respectful of each other and who they are for a healthy relationship to grow. How about communication? Open communication is vital in any relationship to define boundaries. You need it to communicate sentiments, needs, and desires. You need it to resolve conflicts even with regard to intimacy. Without great communication, how can anything in the relationship be clear and the values be reinforced? With open communication, you will define the values and desires for your love life. Having a lifelong relationship takes a gigantic investment of time, energy, and emotion. Extraordinary couples support and develop their communication, their caring affections for one another, and their sexual preferences. They take time to talk confidently to each other and effectively tune in, and they embrace and manage conflict and become familiar with one another's ways of expressing love and affection.

PARENTING

This is a significant exploration for parents and guardians alike; this category is significant because the eventual fate of the entire human race relies upon probably a few of us doing it right. You need to choose what sort of parent you would need to be. According to therapists who study child-rearing, there are four fundamental styles of child-rearing: dictatorial, authoritative, lenient, and unengaged. The styles vary regarding how much inclusion you have in your kid's life and how much control you attempt to apply over your kid's conduct. Being a decent parent implies you have to show your child morality. Setting limits and being consistent are the keys to good discipline. Be kind and firm when enforcing those rules. Focus on the reason behind the child's behavior. Often, things such as your own health or the health of your marriage are kept on the back burner when a child is born. If you don't pay attention to them, they will become bigger problems down the road. Take good care of yourself physically and mentally. Take time to strengthen your relationship with your spouse. If these two areas fail, your child will suffer too.

SOCIAL

Here you will evaluate your relationships with companions, friends, and more distant family. You will come to comprehend which connections contribute decidedly to your life and which relationships drain you. You'll realize what actions you can take to reinforce your most significant connections and what you can do to release unhealthy connections. One of the approaches to assess your relationships with a friend is to see if both of you are equally invested in the friendship. A healthy friendship is balanced, with both people equally invested in the relationship. For example, both friends should take time to call each other or to hang out. If you are doing all the calling and inviting, it could be a sign that this friendship is unhealthy.

CAREER

Explore the meaning and rewards of a great career or vocation. Learn strategies to acquire additional work-related skills to earn a promotion and make more money. Professional achievement means being proactive. To start with, it is a mindset. You have to understand that nobody thinks about your career and its budgetary effect more than you do. If you want professional success, you need to be proactive. Get things going that your boss needs to have done, overperform, and you will get paid more and advance. Be proactive and don't assume that your supervisor knows about how you are overperforming. Your manager is a bustling individual as well and has objectives to achieve, so she probably won't be following your advancement that intently. Performance reviews allow the executives to check whether workers are accomplishing anticipated degrees of execution and to offer them significant feedback, direction, and encouragement. Truly both execution (over-conveying) and being affable are important. Remember that you should treat people the way they want to be treated. Additionally, it is essential that you build up your skill sets and aptitudes. It's a fact of life that having certain skills can improve opportunities to obtain a promotion.

FINANCIAL

This is one of the most important categories. Do you need to know why money is important to you? What will money enable you to accomplish? How can you create wealth and to what end? It is a process of self-discovery and you will view yourself and your financial life in an altogether new manner.

QUALITY OF LIFE

In this category you will determine how you wish to spend the hours, the days, and the years of your life. You will discover how a life well lived can lead to rewarding spiritual, intellectual, and emotional breakthroughs and can improve who you are as a human being as you continue to grow and give back to enhance your community. This category is comprehensive and measures your life satisfaction, including everything from physical health, family, education, employment, wealth, religious beliefs, and finances, to the environment.

LIFE VISION

According to Carl Jung, your vision will become clear only when you can look into your heart: "Who looks outside, dreams; who looks inside, awakes." Keep the words of late mythologist Joseph Campbell in mind and "follow your bliss."

Now that you have gone through the soul-searching process of evaluating each category of your life, you will be in a great position to create and implement a comprehensive plan that includes health and fitness; your financial, intellectual, emotional, spiritual, and social life; your character; your love relationships; your career, etcetera, in order to achieve financial freedom and live your dream life.

13

INVEST BY YOURSELF OR OBTAIN GUIDANCE FROM AN EXPERIENCED FIDUCIARY ADVISOR

"Life is a matter of priority and decision."

— BENJAMIN HARDY

The purpose of this chapter is to warn you to expect the usual obstacles when trying to achieve your financial freedom. If you feel that you are able to create a financial plan and to manage your investments, then more power to you. However, if you are like most financially successful people, you will seek assistance from an investment advisor, tax attorney, accountant, and/or a financial advisor to help you navigate through the various advantages and disadvantages of the array of investments available in the marketplace.

There are a lot of investment choices. The question is, which of these investment choices are best for you at this point in your life? Your investment choices and estate planning requirements are quite different based on your age. While you are still young, you need growth and appreciation in your investment portfolio. As you get older, you will become more conservative with estate planning and tax-advantage investments.

You will fail with money and will not achieve financial freedom if you spend money beyond your means, don't have a financial plan, do not prepare for financial emergencies, and do not invest regularly with a long-term perspective. The time to start a financial plan is now. If you do not start your financial plan now, you will have to take on a bigger savings burden, retire later, or plan for a retirement of financial frugality. Also, you are at risk of selecting investment strategies that are not suited for you based on your overall financial goals. Risky investments and/or lack of investment discipline can also be obstacles to achieving financial well-being. A good example would be an investor who did not diversify her portfolio and lost money due to lack of investment diversification and asset allocation.

If you truly want to reach financial stability, you should know what mistakes not to make, including having a lot of credit card debt with high interest rates and paying the minimum monthly payment or being unable to make minimum payments. Overspending will lead you to a mountain of debt and will make it almost impossible to attain financial stability. Likewise, not saving and investing your money is almost always something that will destroy the prospect of reaching financial stability. In my opinion, the biggest reason for financial failure is not having financial goals. You must take time to write out things that you want to accomplish in the short term and in the long term.

Should you manage your investment portfolio, or should you hire a fiduciary advisor? Frequently, it makes sense to hire a fiduciary advisor when you have a high net worth, you are planning to start a family, or you are nearing retirement. High-net-worth individuals need advance estate and tax planning strategies. If you are planning to start a family, you will need to know how best to manage the new costs of having children and think about life insurance, estate planning, and college savings for the first time. If you are planning to retire, there are important financial questions that retirees must answer: am I financially ready to retire? How and when should I file for Social Security? What is the best strategy for withdrawing funds to both meet my needs and make my money last? All these questions have a big impact on your retirement lifestyle and none of them are easy to answer on your own.

A good fiduciary advisor will help you navigate and prioritize all these responsibilities so that you can create a secure and enjoyable life for your family, both today and in the future. There are two main ways fiduciary advisors are compensated: through client fees, usually charged either on an hourly basis or as a percentage of client assets under management, or through commissions for certain financial transactions, such as the sale of insurance products. If you decide to hire a fiduciary advisor, make sure that the fiduciary advisor is registered with the state or SEC and that your money is held with a reputable third-party custodian such as Schwab, TD Ameritrade, or Fidelity, which offers 24/7 online account access and sends the monthly statements directly to you.

Remember, it all starts with you. Know what you want in life and identify your priorities. If you desire to hire a fiduciary advisor, she can help you achieve your financial goals and achieve financial freedom to enable you to enjoy your dream life.

14

WHAT DOES IT FEEL LIKE HAVING FINANCIAL WELL-BEING?

"After you become a millionaire, you can give all of your money away because what's important is not the million dollars; what's important is the person you have become in the process of becoming a millionaire."

— JIM ROHN

I trust that you will take time to read and implement some of the ideas identified in this book. You must decide whether you want to navigate to financial freedom on your own or whether you should hire an experienced fiduciary advisor to help you create a financial plan, implement a budget, and create a short- and/or long-term plan to achieve your desired outcome. The earlier you start planning and investing to achieve your financial freedom, the greater the odds that you will achieve it. The time to take action is now. If you are reading this book, I know that you are ready to start a financial plan to achieve financial freedom, to live the lifestyle you always dreamed of, and to avail yourself of life choices leading to total fulfillment and happiness.

It is important to create a financial plan and do self-analysis to get clear about your short- and long-term financial goals. You will begin by taking a detailed inventory of your financial situation. It is important to be able to define your financial goals and objectives, your risk profile, and the time frame needed to invest money so that you will not get stuck working forever. Creating and committing to a monthly budget is imperative to enable you to manage your monthly income and expenses.

You will need to thoughtfully identify your financial goals and fund them with a committed monthly investment. Whether you manage your own portfolio or hire a fiduciary advisor, you need to actively review your investment portfolio frequently throughout the year to make portfolio adjustments for your desired portfolio growth and capital appreciation. It is important to have a diversified portfolio such as a balanced mutual fund that contains a stock component, a bond component, and sometimes a money market component in a single portfolio. Generally, these mutual funds stick to a relatively fixed mix of stocks and bonds. Other investment alternatives are great choices depending on your risk profile and time horizon. For instance, an investment alternative could be a professionally managed trust that pools the savings of many investors and invests them in securities like stocks, bonds, short-term money market instruments, and commodities, including precious metals.

There are also many investment alternatives when planning for retirement. You will also need to know when to invest in annuities and insurance, including long-term care. Having a sense of your life expectancy can mean the difference between investing success and failure.

One of the primary drives of a successful portfolio strategy is the ability to identify the investment time horizon for your assets. Let me know if you need help creating your financial plan; in the meantime, I wish you much success in achieving your financial freedom by creating and adhering to your financial plan. I trust that you will take time to read and implement some of the ideas identified in this book. In closing, my wish for you is that you, like Ms. Maven, feel happy and secure in your financial future and that you move forward with confidence and make choices that enable you to achieve your financial freedom and enjoy your life.

ACKNOWLEDGMENTS

I have known since I was a little girl that I had a strong desire for financial freedom. I always wanted to be verbally articulate like my dad, who was a poet. I also wanted to be as industrious as my mother, who owned a small business. They were born in Guayaquil, Ecuador and came to the United States, the land of opportunity, in 1970. They both gifted some of their talents to me, and this book is a physical manifestation of my love and gratitude for my parents.

Writing to promote pay equity and education for women and girls is one thing. However, committing to completing a book from cover to cover is a level up from the day-to-day writing that I am used to. I found time during the 2020 pandemic to write this book to provide a road map to financial freedom for those people seeking to achieve financial freedom. I have often heard that "when the student is ready, the teacher will appear." That was another welcome synchronicity with me to find my writing coach, Angela Lauria, through The Author's Way. Special thanks again to Angela, CEO and founder of The Author Incubator, for believing in me and my message. To my developmental editor, Andrae Smith Jr., and managing editor, Cory Hott, thanks for making the process seamless and easy.

I cannot express enough gratitude for Benjamin Hardy, Jim Rohn, Zig Ziglar, Oprah Winfrey, Wayne Dyer, and Abraham Hicks. Until I studied their teachings, I had no idea that I had any amount of control over my thoughts, emotions, and my life. Special thanks to the American Association of University Women members, and college and university partners. I am so appreciative of the endless opportunities that I have been given as a member of the team to promote pay equity and education for women and girls. Not only did I gain tremendous experience and knowledge while working with you, but I also developed the deepest and dearest friendships with my colleagues. I would love to name you all here but given my twenty-plus years in New York State, that would require an entirely separate book. I will shout out to a few special people: Tony Robbins, Kimberly Churches, Charles Flynn, Hajtejah Schaefer, Dr. Gunatheesan Namasivayam, Juan Felix Rossetti, Leo Benvenuto, Mo Anderson, Sawsan

Gheith, and Dinni Gordon, who have earned my love and respect for eternity.

Many thanks to my life coach, Vishen Lakhiani at Mindvalley University, and his team of teachers and coaches, including Robin Sharma, Emily Fletcher, Michael Beckwith, and Jon and Missy Butcher. There are not words to thank you for how you have impacted my life. You welcomed me, coached me, and believed in me. To my tribe and friends, thank you for taking time to follow my work and spread my message to achieve financial freedom. It is an honor to serve you in the largest capacity I can, and I appreciate the opportunity to support clients with massive breakthroughs. I genuinely love helping other people see their power. It is a joy that has no words to describe it. It fills my heart to the brim to hear stories of emotional transformation. Carry on, brave souls. You were meant for this work. Together, we can bring financial freedom.

To my family, I thank you for allowing me to be myself. My husband, Stephen, and my sons, Michael and Tommy, are my biggest fans – always have been, and always will be. I love and appreciate them so much. Thank you to my sons' respective wives, Dominique and Kathryn. This book is dedicated to my first granddaughter, Ms. Maven Rose. May you all learn to live a joyful and happy life under all circumstances of life. My brothers, Francisco, Sergio, Ruben, and Eloy, and my sister, Zulema, are my proudest fans – seeing them beam with pride over my accomplishments and having them text me encouraging thoughts means a lot to me. Thank you for your patience and for your unconditional love. Thank you for your sense of humor, gentleness, acceptance, and love.

To my Harvard Business School/OPM32 friends or, as I lovingly refer to them, The Old Guard, my gratefulness for our seventeen-plus years of friendship as OPMers, colleagues, and friends has no bounds. We were a powerhouse team then and we are a powerhouse team today. We are a team for life. So much love and appreciation for you all. Finally, special thanks to Gary Keller, entrepreneur, author, and founder of Keller Williams Realty International, the largest real estate company in the world. Gary's love and kindness are a great model for all business owners to follow. I will leave you with one final thought, one of Gary's quotes: "Don't let small thinking cut your life down to size. Think big, aim high, act bold, and see just how big you can blow up your life."

My gratitude extends to my mentors, mentees, and colleagues and friends who have worked closely with me in our striving to achieve pay equity and education for women and girls: to Kathryn Swintek Dorra, Le Hoa Wysham, Benjamin Hardy, Nada Anid, Marta Panero, Gunatheesan Navasivayam, Jennifer McDonald, Dr. C.S. Rani, Nancy Mion, Dr.

Jessica Sims, Emmelina DeFeo, Estelle Kone, Bolor Amgalan, Valerie Streit, Rowena Lobo, Whitney Bagge, Gloria Abrams, and Sharada Jayapopal, as well as my amazing friends, who are too numerous to mention.

ABOUT THE AUTHOR

Maria L. Ellis, MBA, works with high-net-worth individuals and global family offices around the world. She specializes in banking and real estate investments to maximize cash flow and market appreciation. For more than twenty-five years, Maria has worked for banking, investment, insurance, and real estate companies such as Bank of America, Citibank/Citicorp Investment Services, Gruntal & Co., and Northwestern Mutual. As a trusted global advisor and real estate expert, she currently works at Keller Williams in the Palm Beaches/Miami area and New York City.

Maria is a graduate of the Harvard Business School, Owner/President Management Program. She obtained her BBA and MBA at the University of Massachusetts.

Maria has worked on board leadership positions at the College of Mount Saint Vincent, the American Association of University Women, AAUW NYS, Empire State NYC Branch, the Virginia Gildersleeve International Fund and the Harvard Club of New York City. Maria is also a pro-bono consultant at the Harvard Business School Club of New York City Community Partners and applies her business skills to a variety of topics including strategic planning, marketing, finance, governance, and organizational development.

Maria has been married for thirty-six years to Stephen W. Ellis, with whom she has two sons, Michael S. Ellis, and Thomas W. Ellis.

ABOUT DIFFERENCE PRESS

Difference Press is the exclusive publishing arm of The Author Incubator, an educational company for entrepreneurs – including life coaches, healers, consultants, and community leaders – looking for a comprehensive solution to get their books written, published, and promoted. Its founder, Dr. Angela Lauria, has been bringing to life the literary ventures of hundreds of authors-in-transformation since 1994.

A boutique-style self-publishing service for clients of The Author Incubator, Difference Press boasts a fair and easy-to-understand profit structure, low-priced author copies, and author-friendly contract terms. Most importantly, all of our #incubatedauthors maintain ownership of their copyright at all times.

LET'S START A MOVEMENT WITH YOUR MESSAGE

In a market where hundreds of thousands of books are published every year and are never heard from again, The Author Incubator is different. Not only do all Difference Press books reach Amazon bestseller status, but all of our authors are actively changing lives and making a difference.

Since launching in 2013, we've served over 500 authors who came to us with an idea for a book and were able to write it and get it self-published in less than 6 months. In addition, more than 100 of those books were picked up by traditional publishers and are now available in bookstores. We do this by selecting the highest quality and highest potential applicants for our future programs.

Our program doesn't only teach you how to write a book – our team of coaches, developmental editors, copy editors, art directors, and marketing experts incubate you from having a book idea to being a published, bestselling author, ensuring that the book you create can actually make a difference in the world. Then we give you the training you need to use your book to make the difference in the world, or to create a business out of serving your readers.

ARE YOU READY TO MAKE A DIFFERENCE?

You've seen other people make a difference with a book. Now it's your turn. If you are ready to stop watching and start taking massive action, go to http://theauthorincubator.com/apply/.

"Yes, I'm ready!"

OTHER BOOKS BY DIFFERENCE PRESS

The Inspirational Business: A Nine-Step Guide to Building a Business That Makes a Difference and Creates a Better Life for Your Family by Avis R. Doctor

Why Do They Always Break up with Me?: The Ultimate Guide to Overcome Heartbreak for Good by Carrie Jeroslow

Virtual Teaching Survival Guide: Strategies for Thriving as a Teacher Using Powerful Tools You Already Have by Cynthia P. King

Strength to Stand above the Crowd: The Soul Safe Project: Part One by Adrienne Lindsey

Revolutionary Weight Loss: The Predictable Plan to Lose It for Good This Time by Kate Motz

Steal Your Skills from Corporate: Use Your Professional Talents to Become an Independent Contractor by Katrina Roddy

Heal Your TBI: The 7-Step Approach for Recovering from a Traumatic Brain Injury by Gail Waitkun

THANK YOU

I would like to thank you for reading my book, which I wrote with you in mind. It is my deepest desire that you have learned the basic investment strategies, that you take action and follow the road map to financial success. Therefore, I am offering you a complimentary financial planning consultation. You may reach me by emailing me at mellis@fsacap.com. Thank you again!